ANTIQUE BOTANICALS II
AN ADULT COLORING BOOK

What makes our books unique & different from all the others?

We're the only adult coloring book publisher who uses original antique botanical art in our books. Over the years we've acquired an extensive collection and we're excited to share it with you.

We're also the only publisher who can show you images of the original antique art which you can use as a reference for your coloration. Visit the Book Images section of our website at http://www.BotanicalArtDesigns.com and click on the cover image of the book you have purchased. You'll be presented with a PDF of the original color images (in as found condition) to use as references as you color.

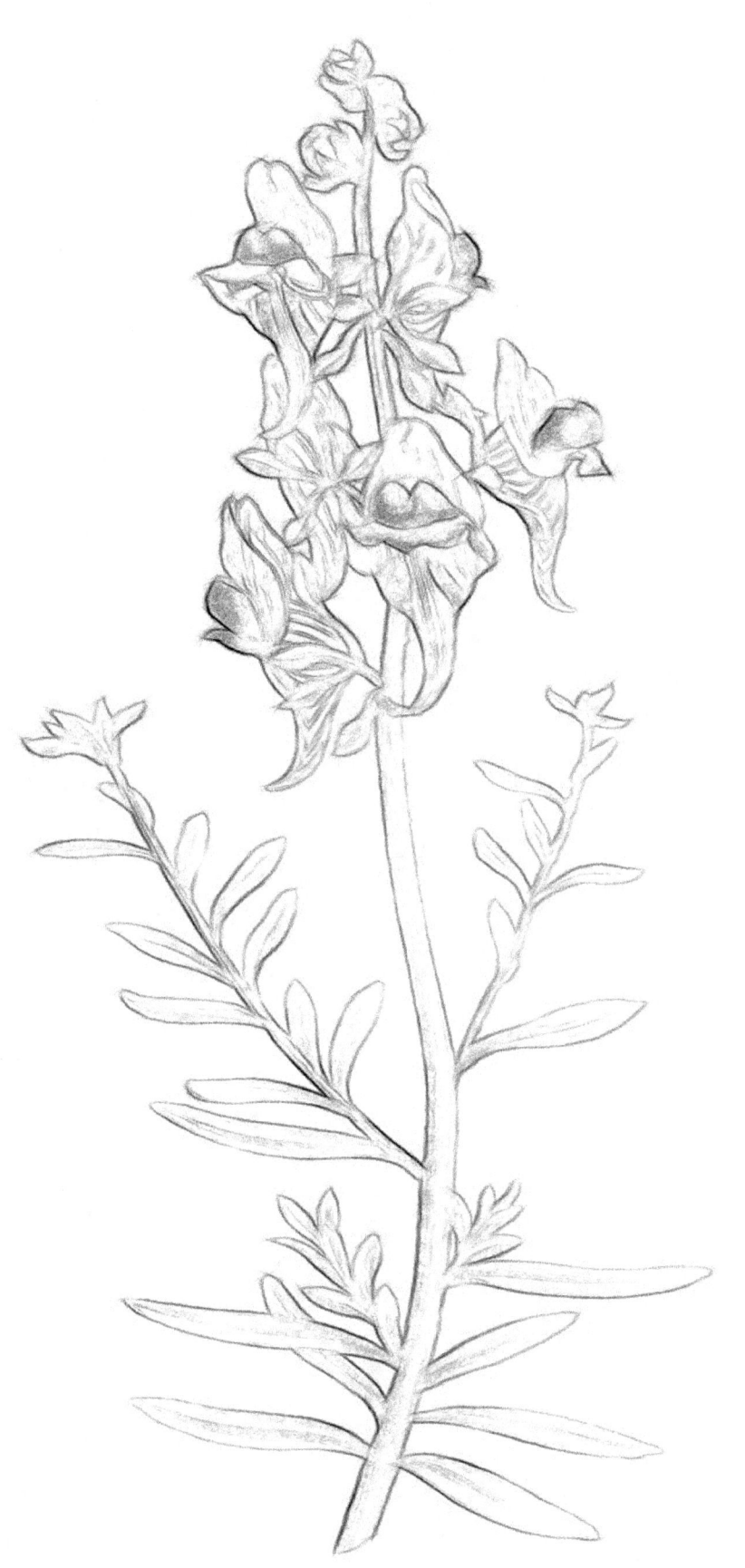

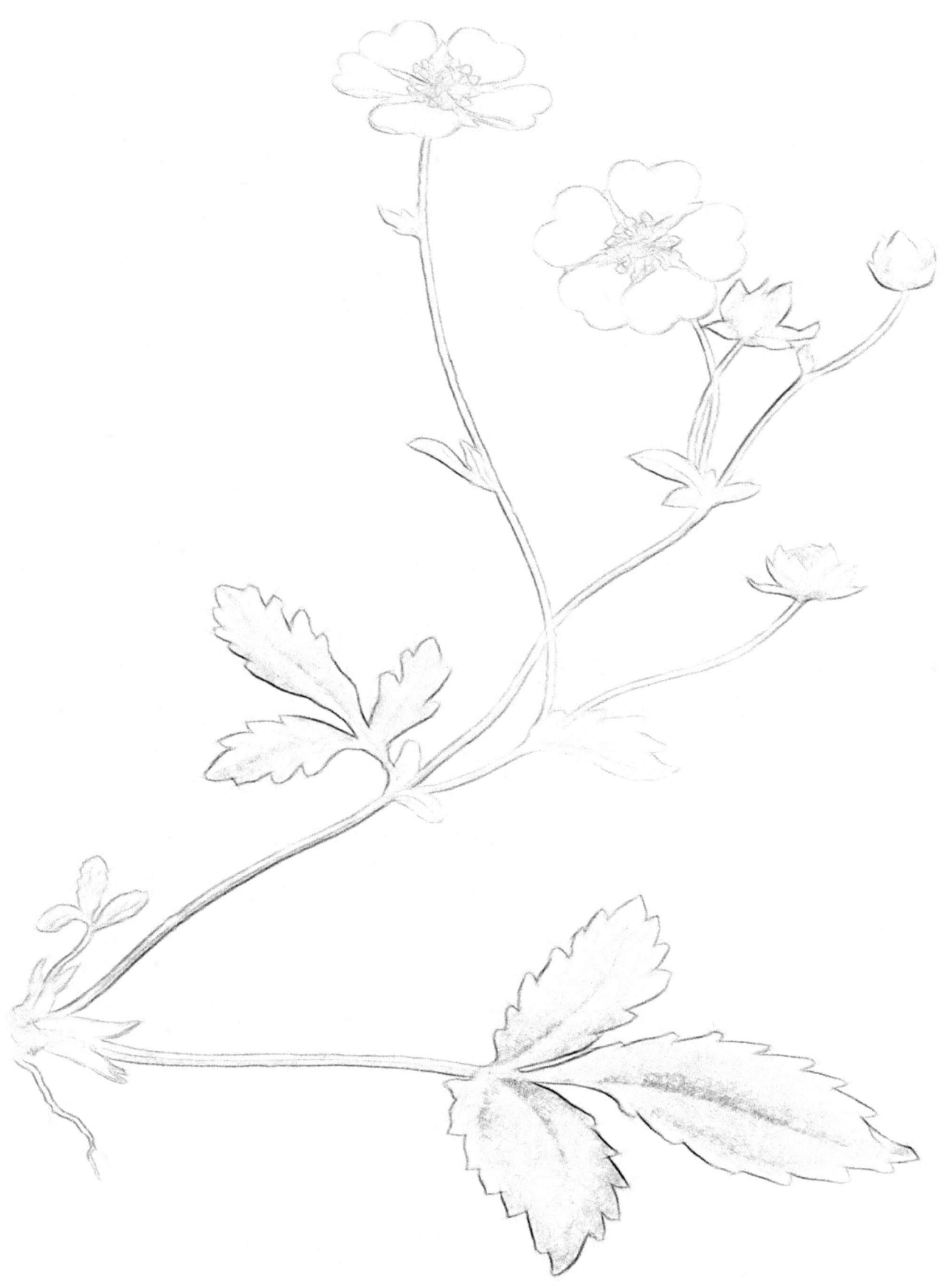

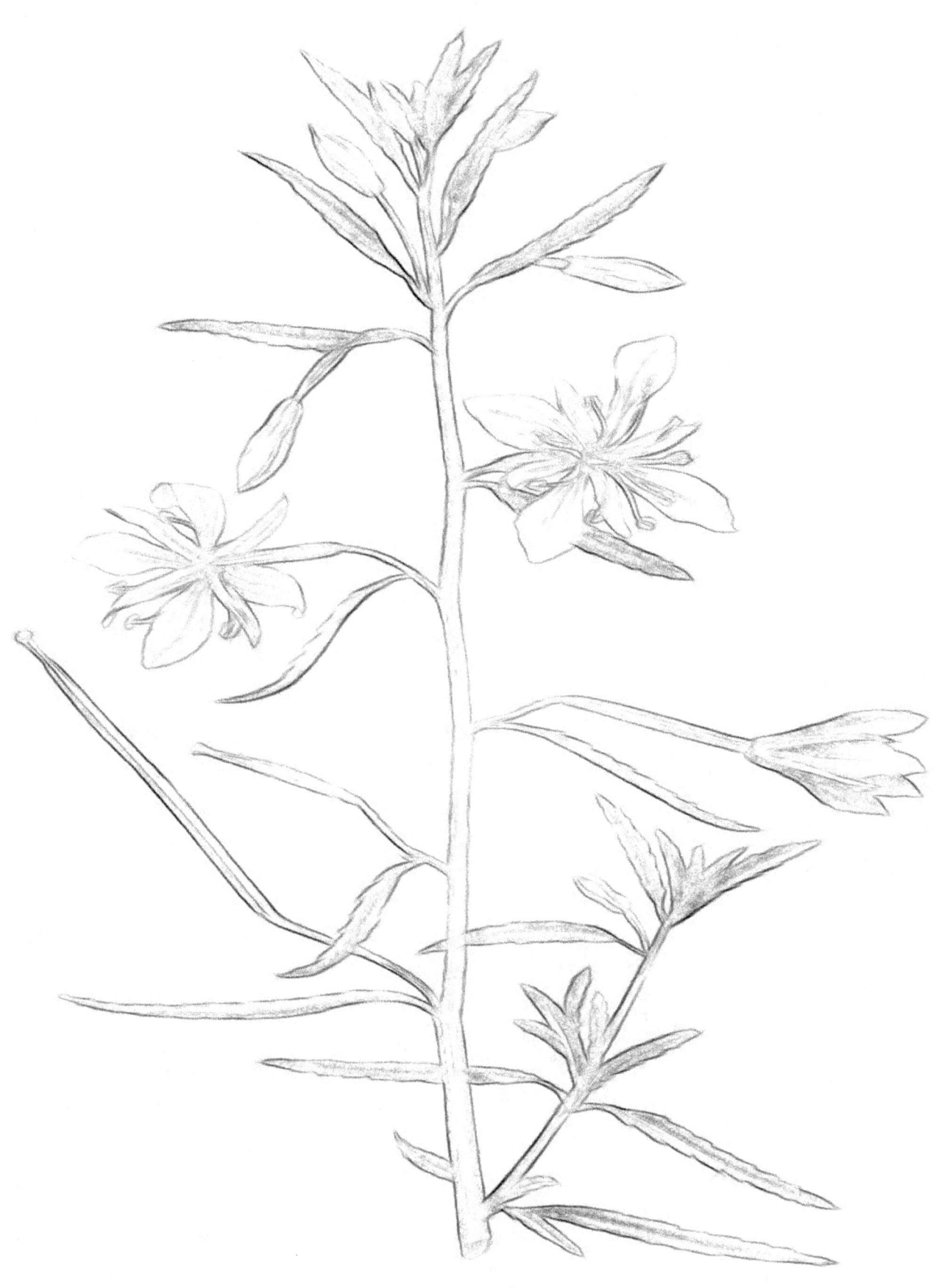

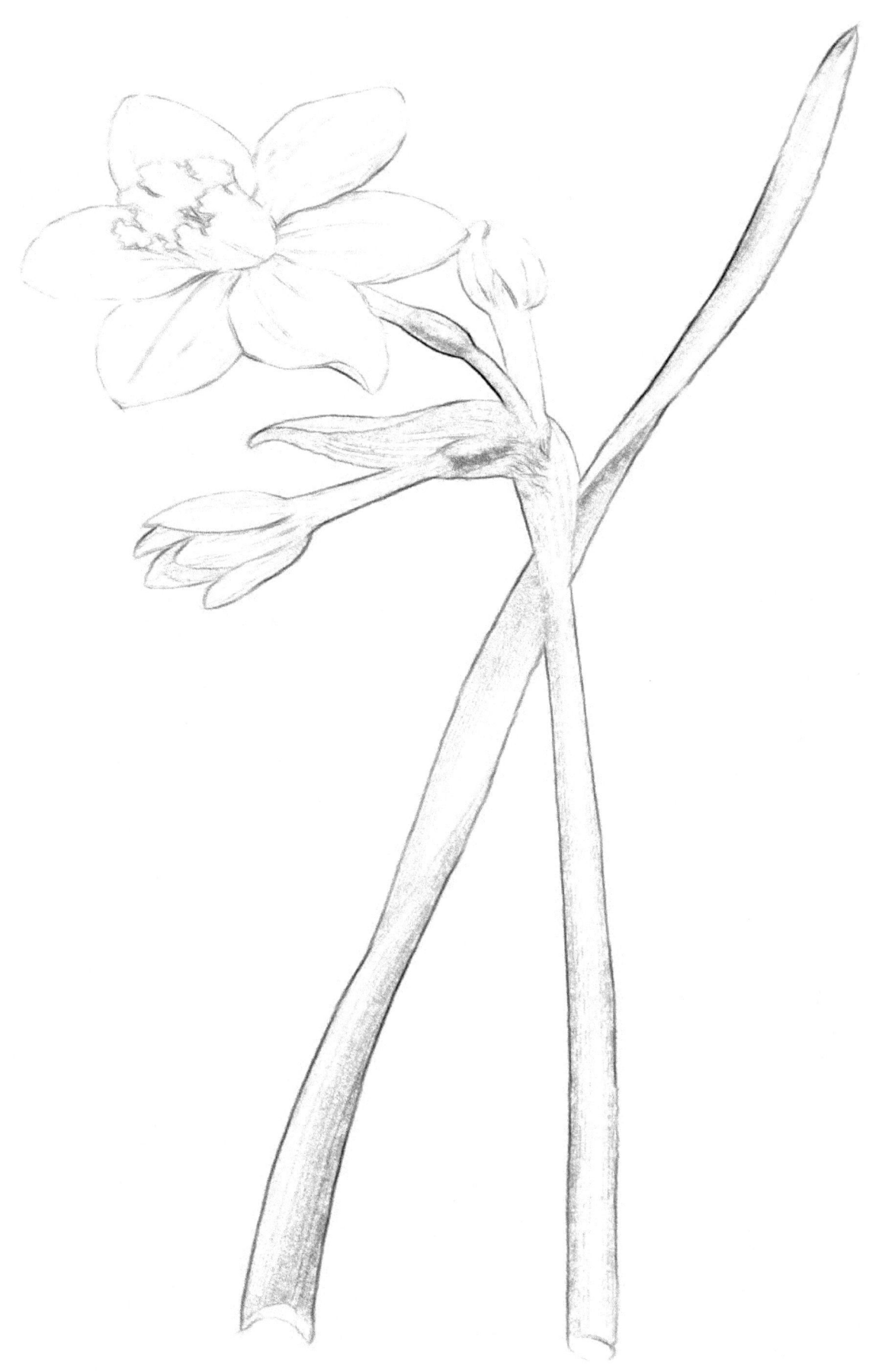

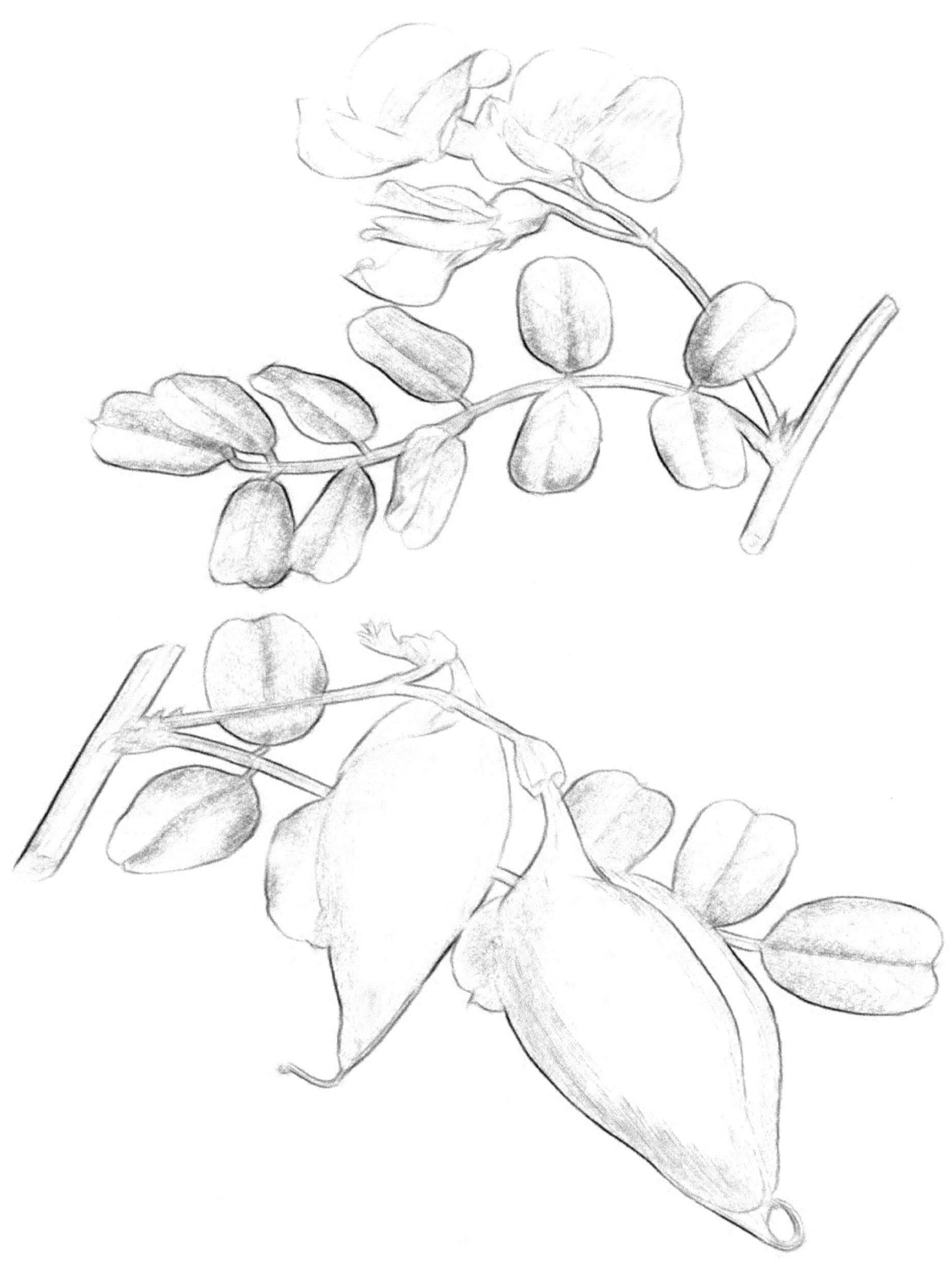

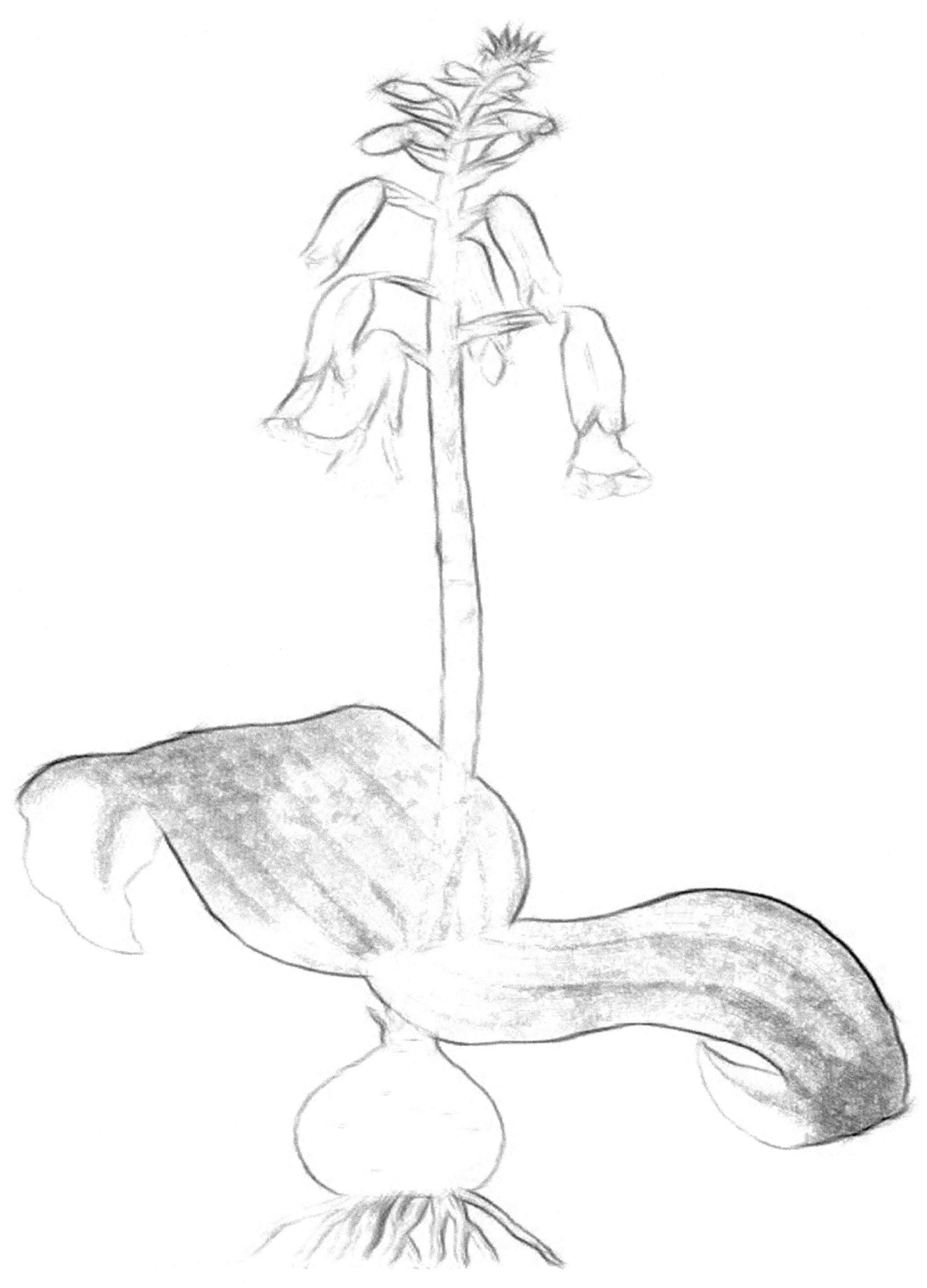

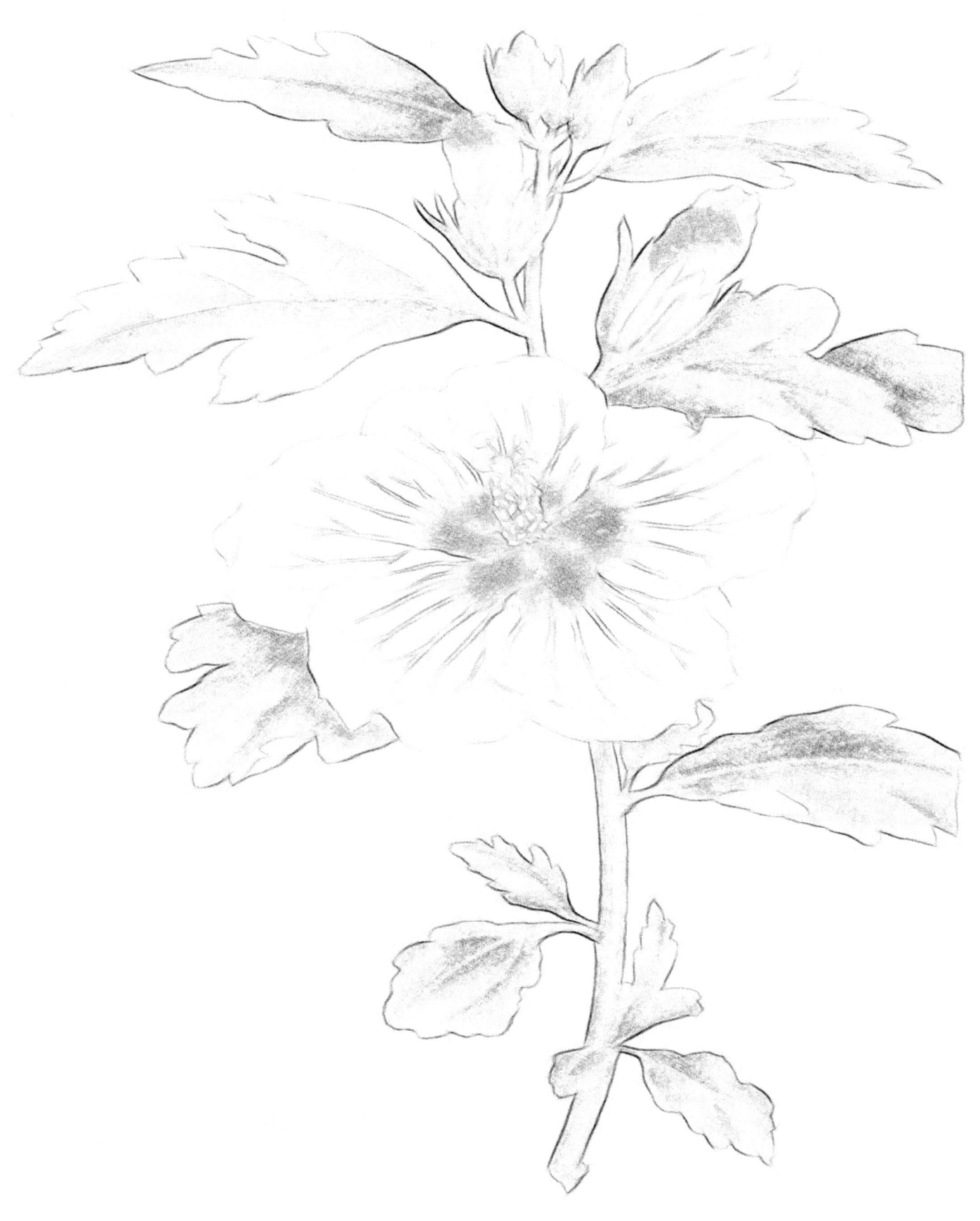

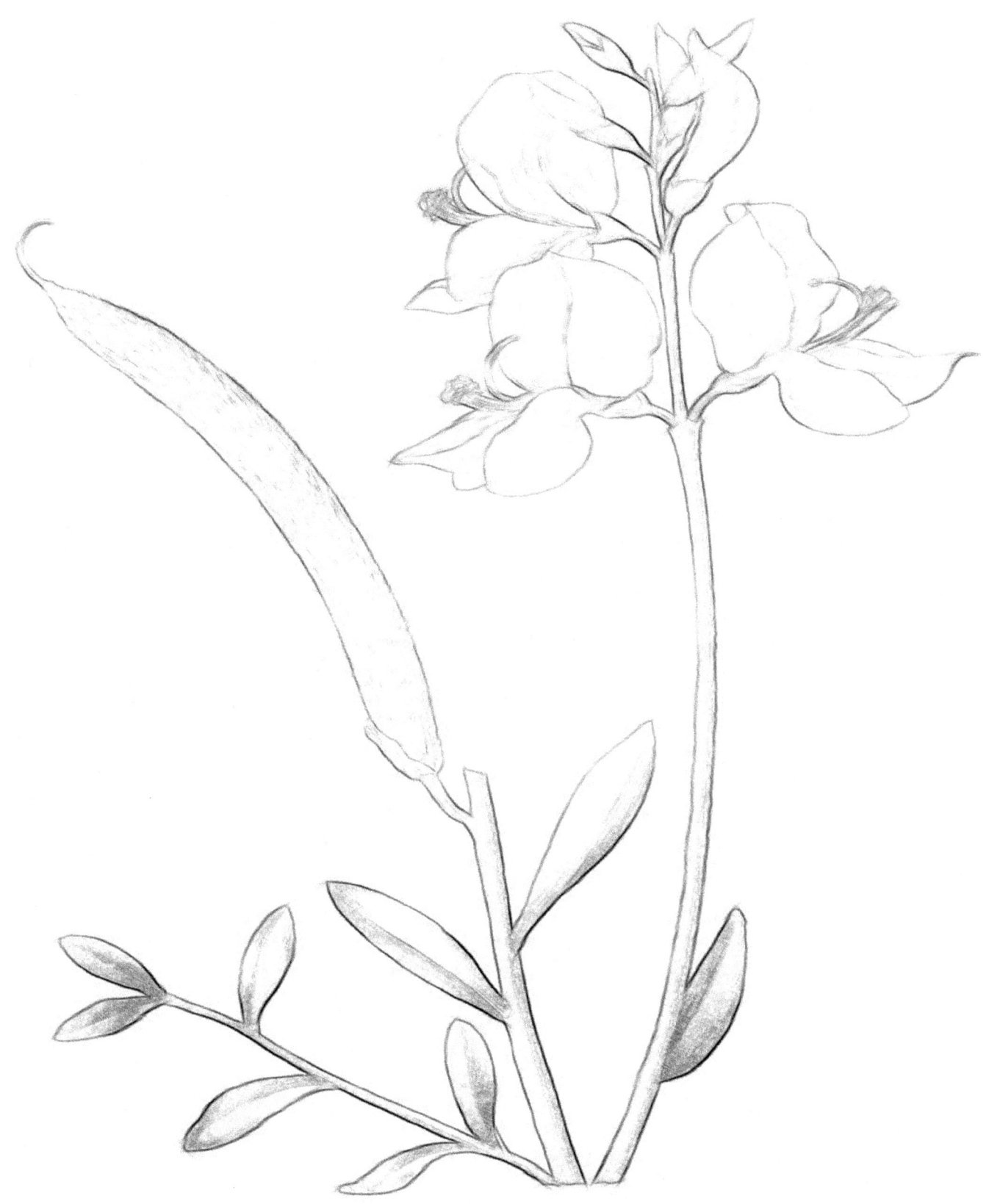

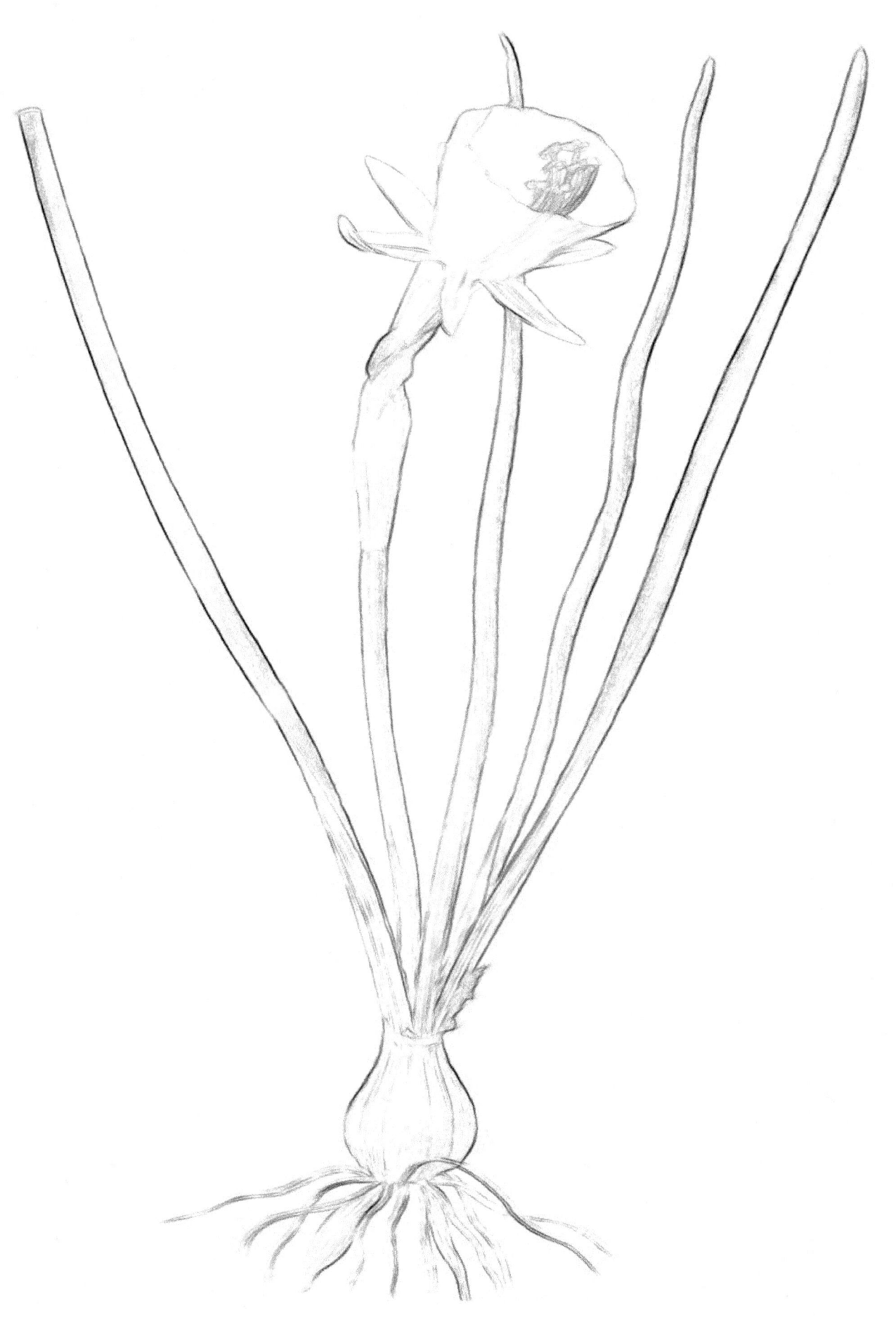

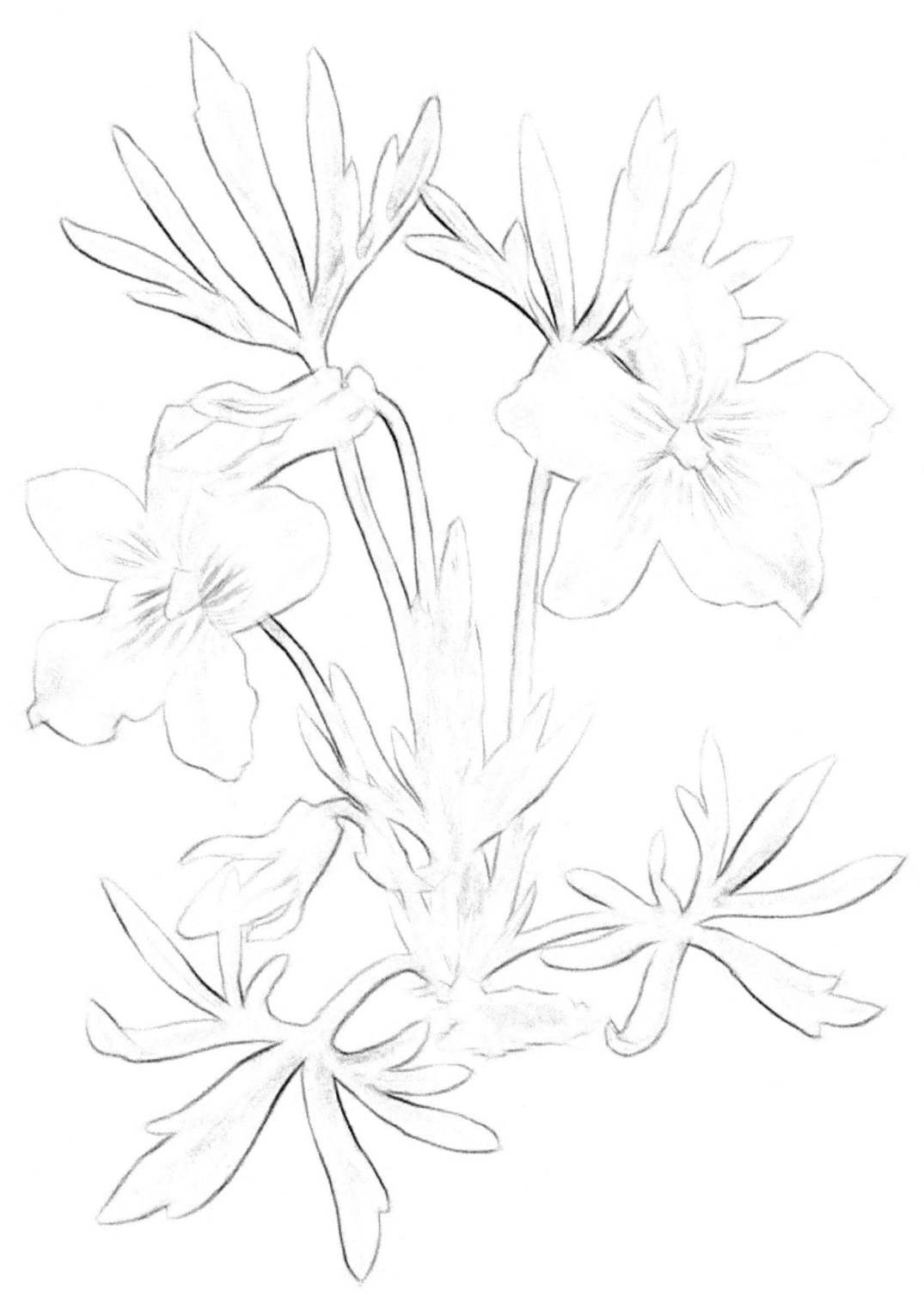

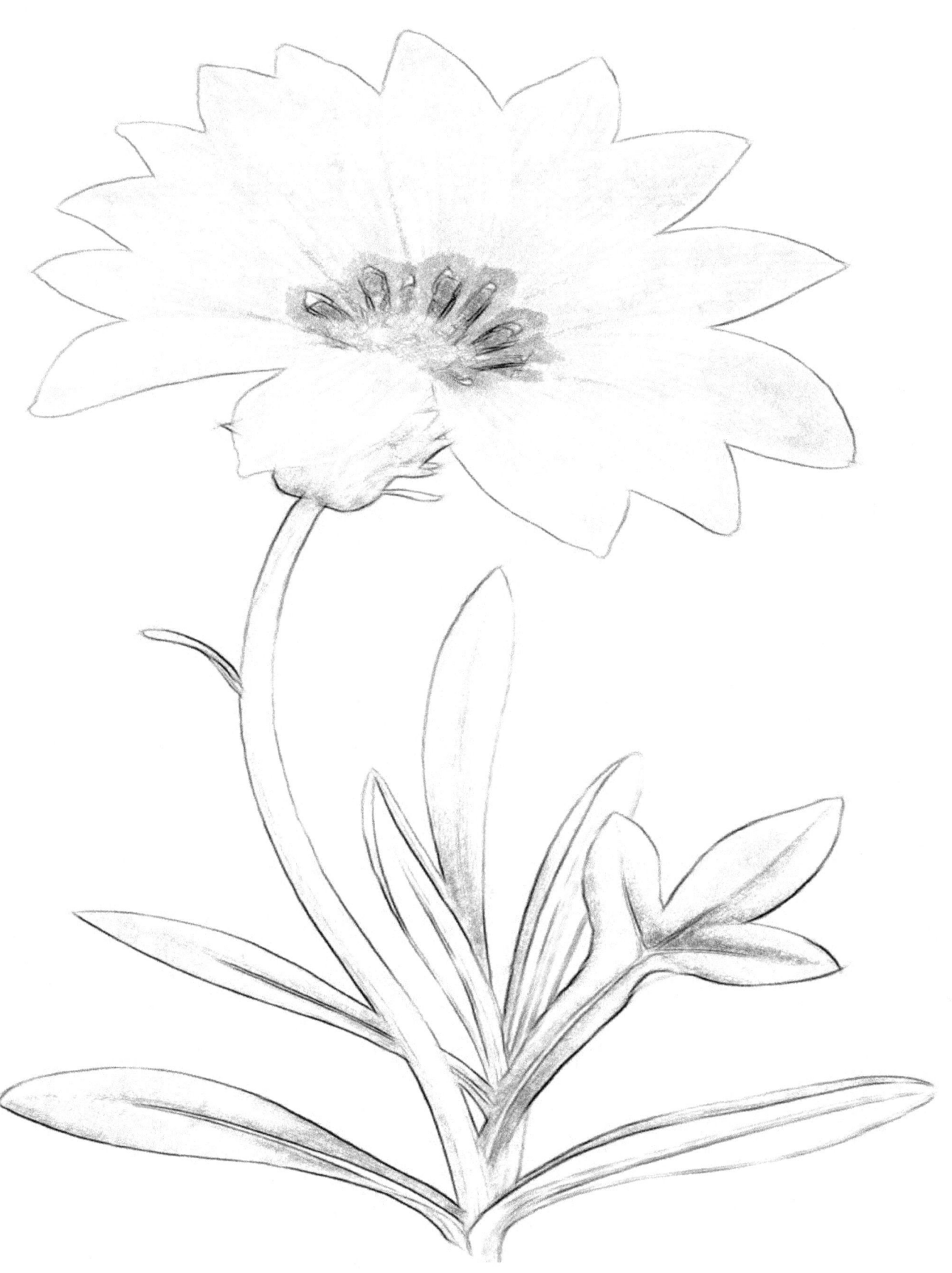

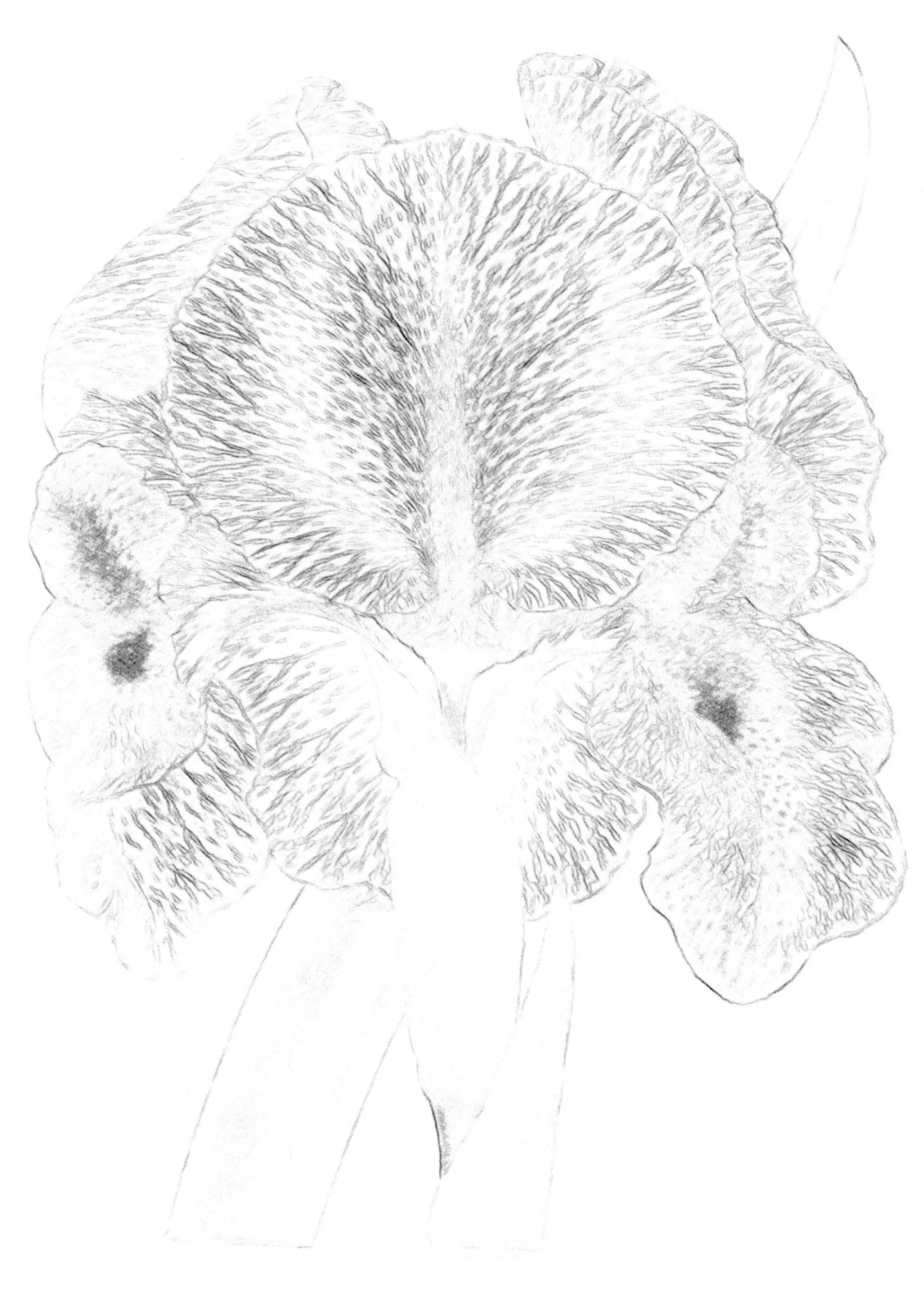

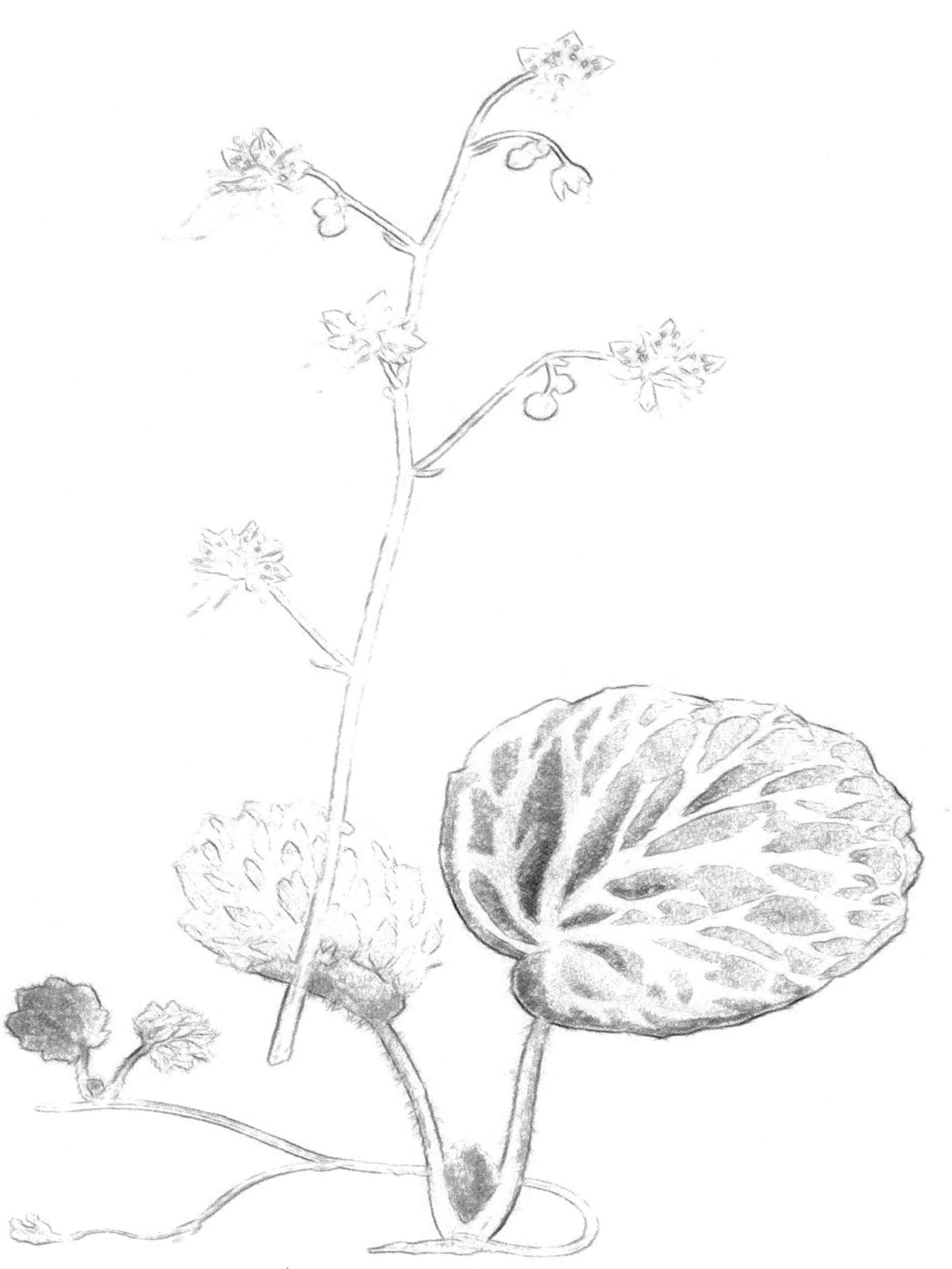

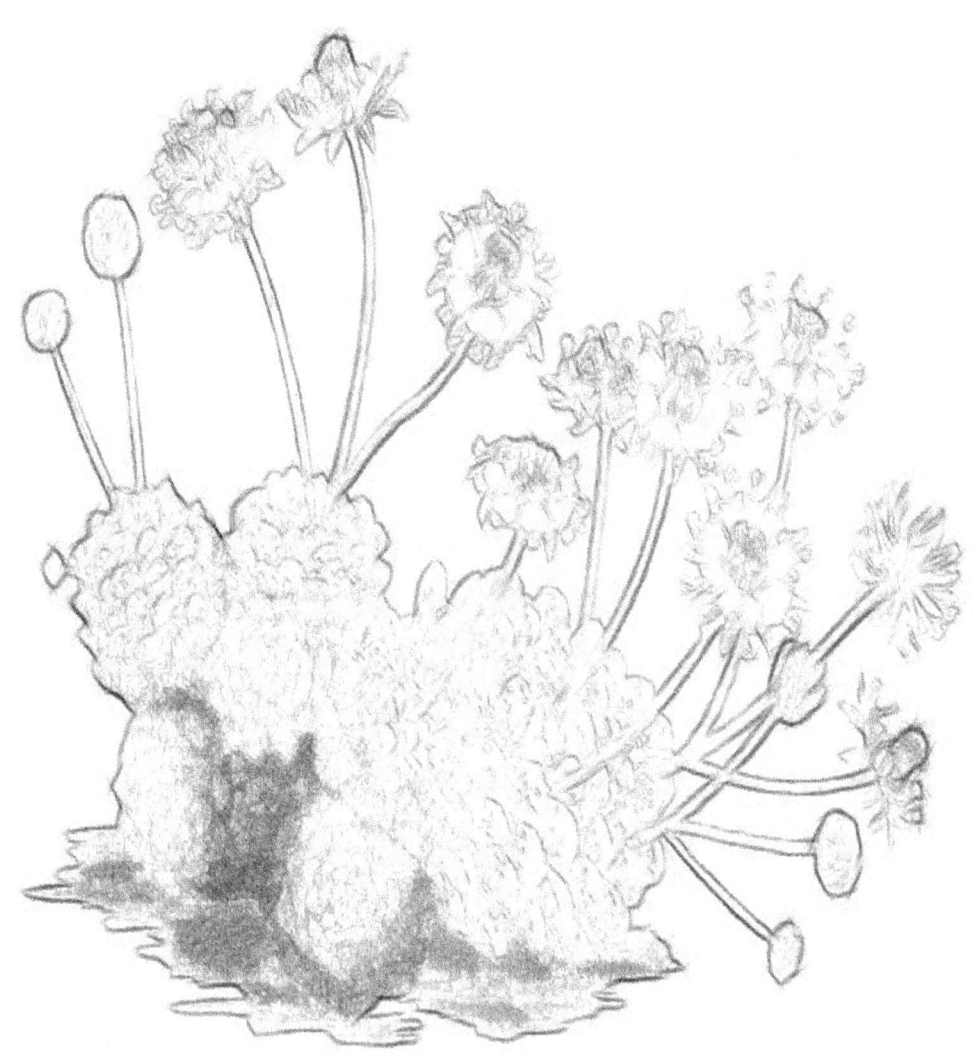

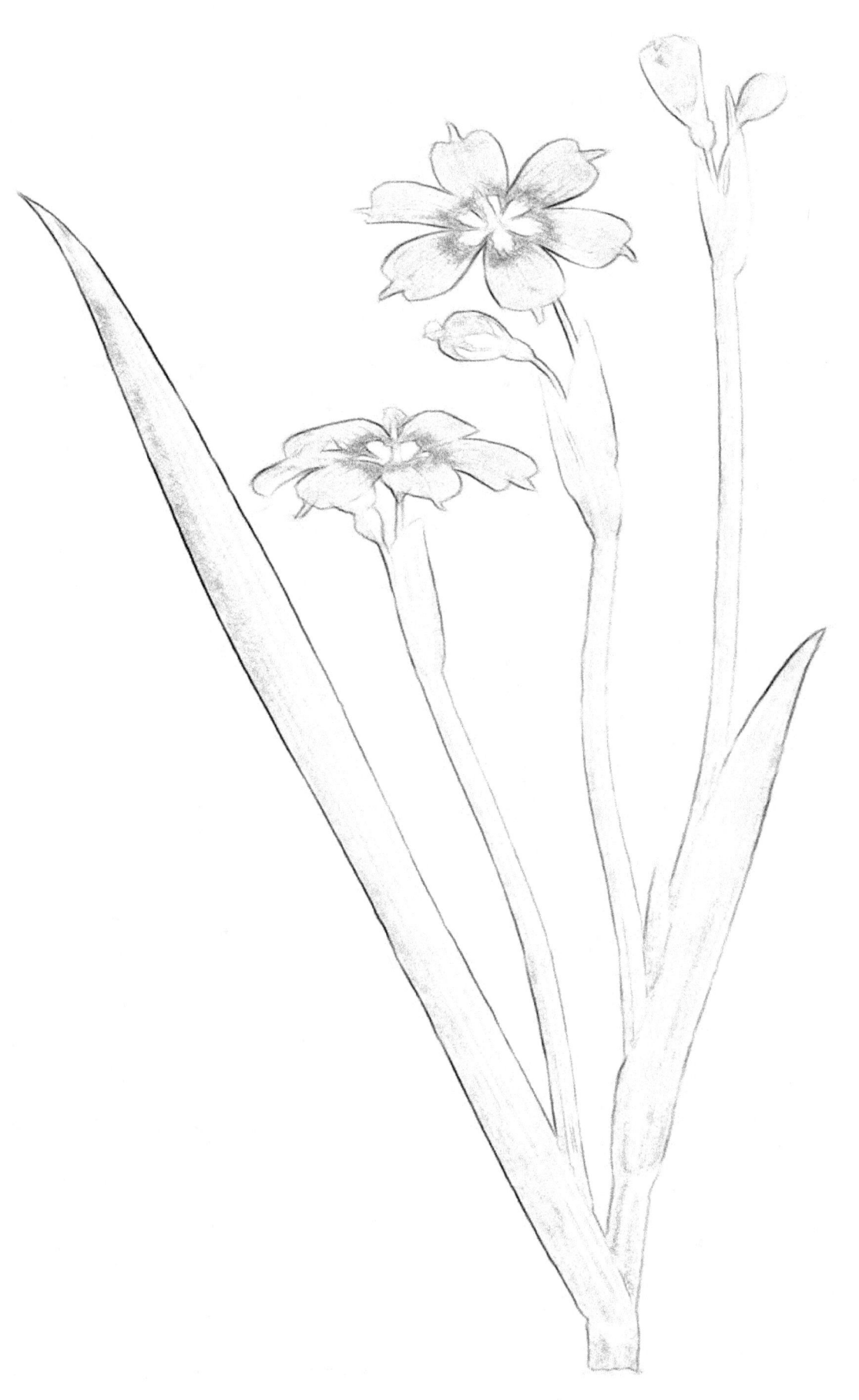

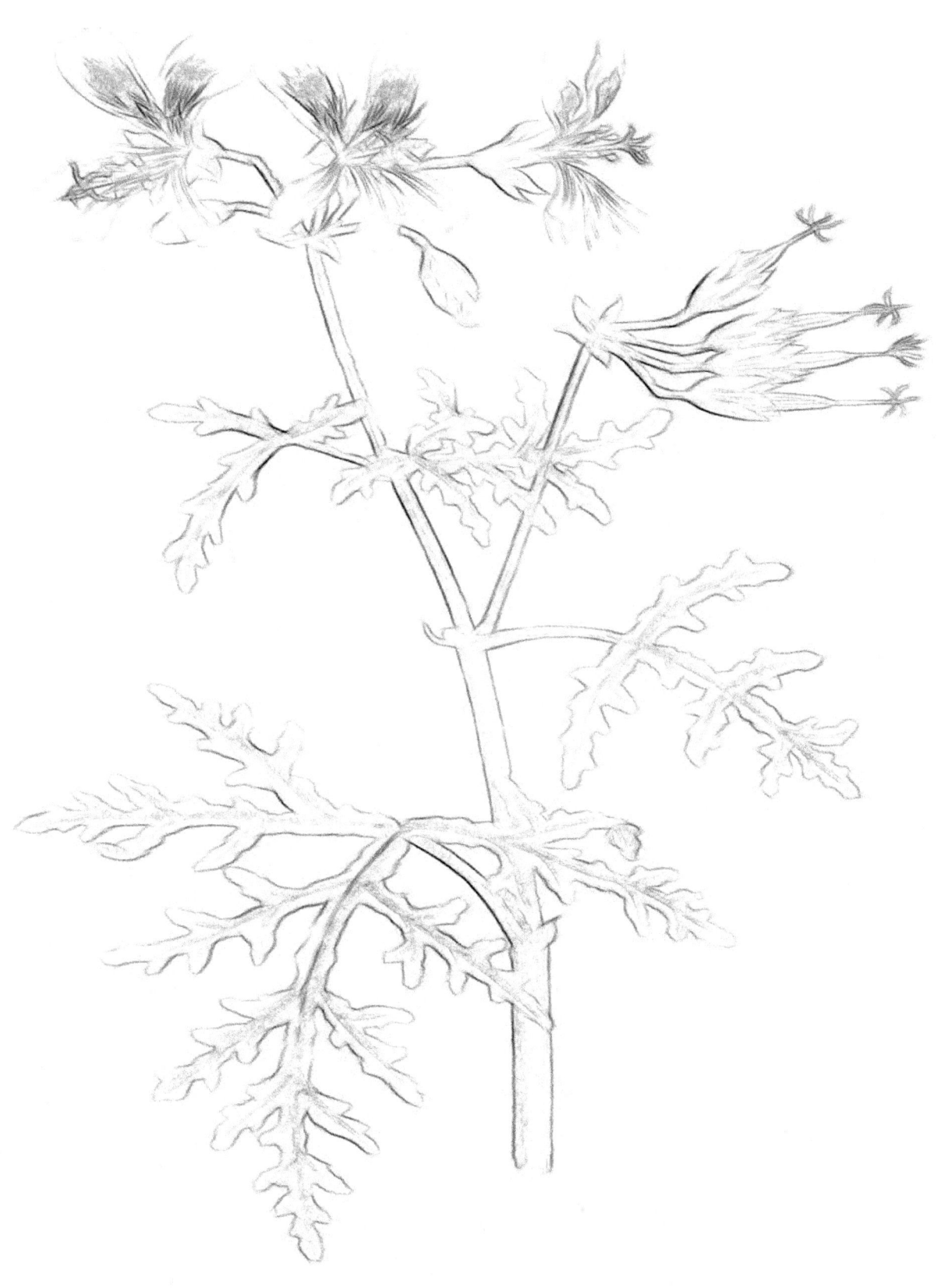

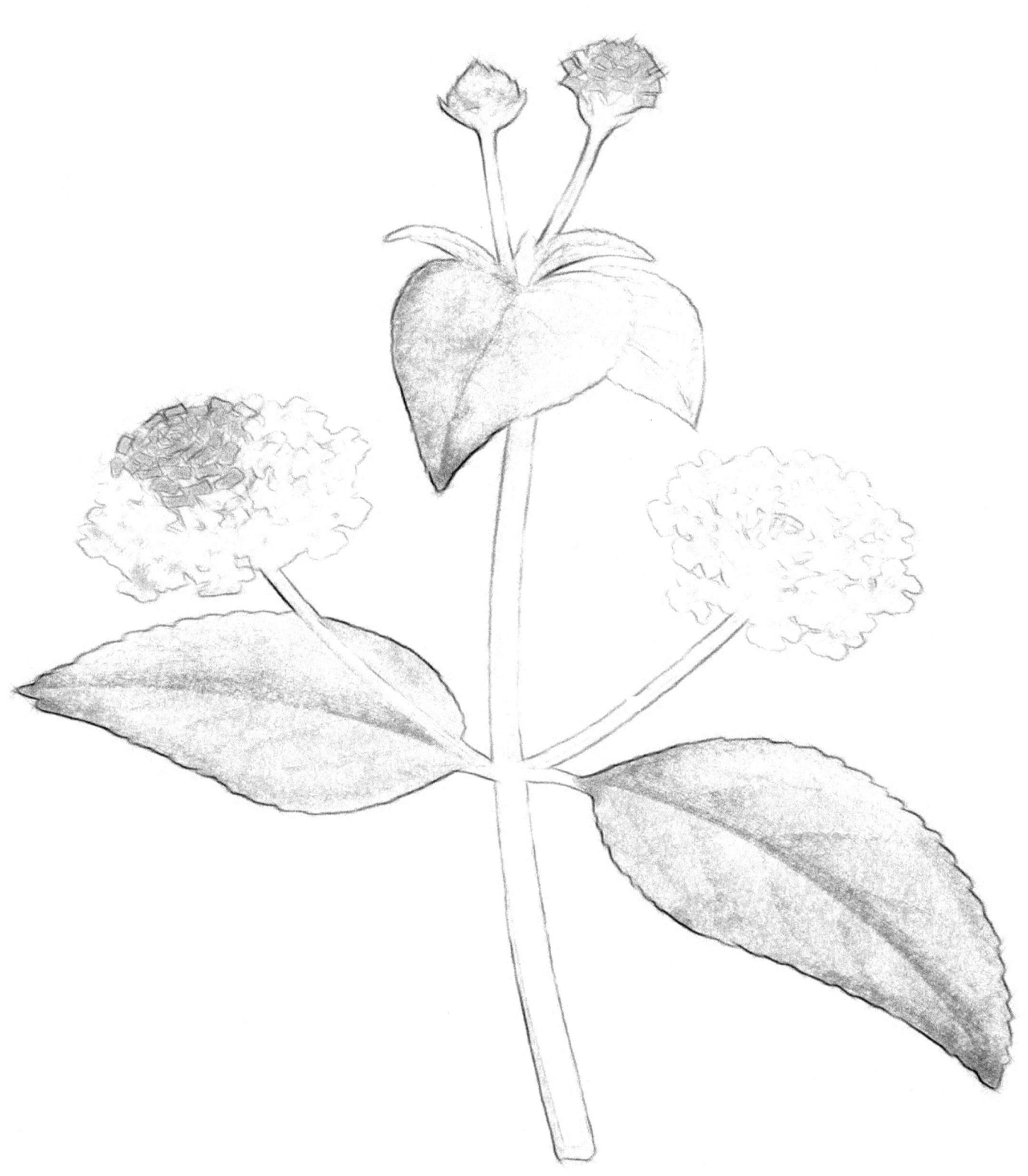

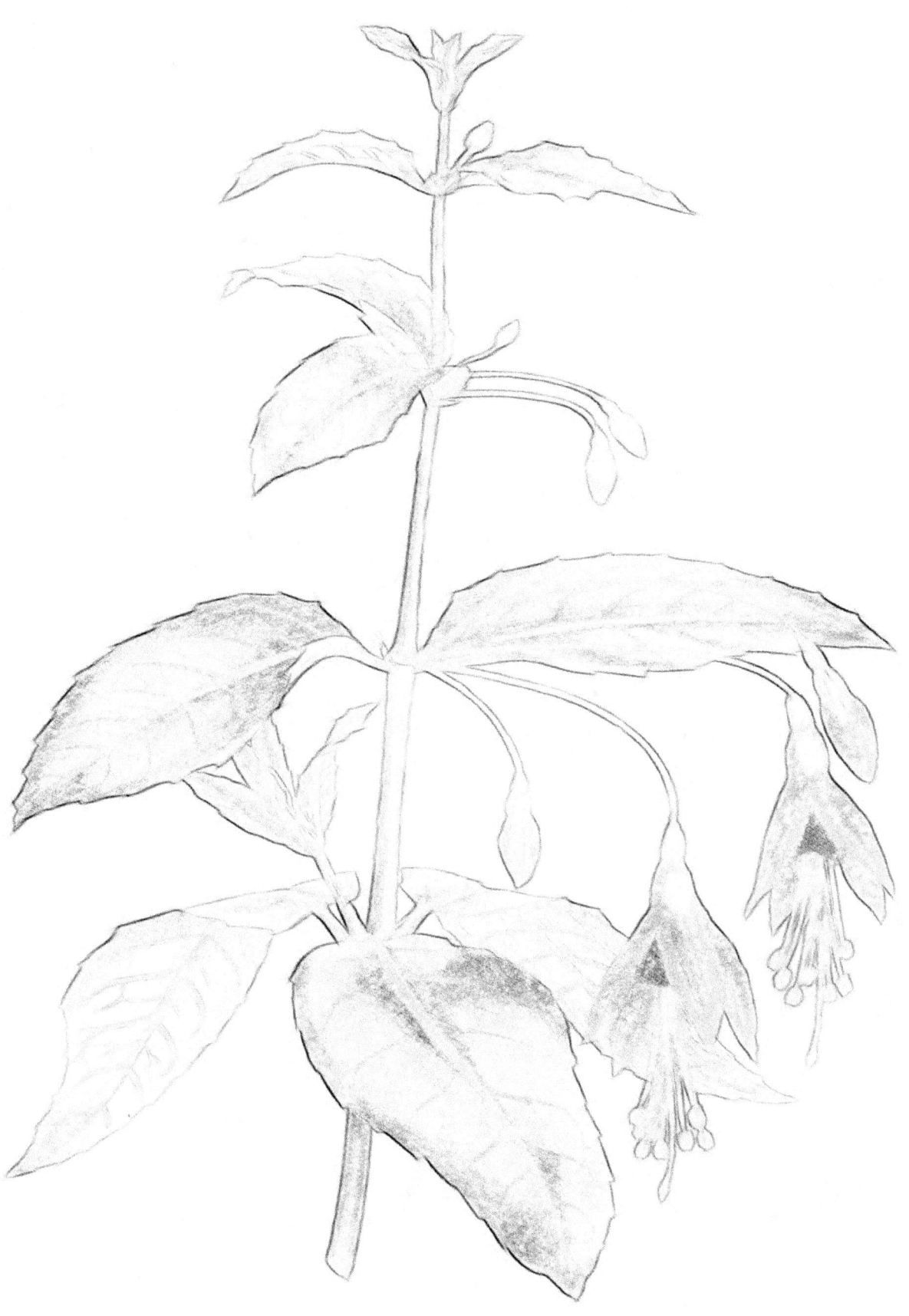

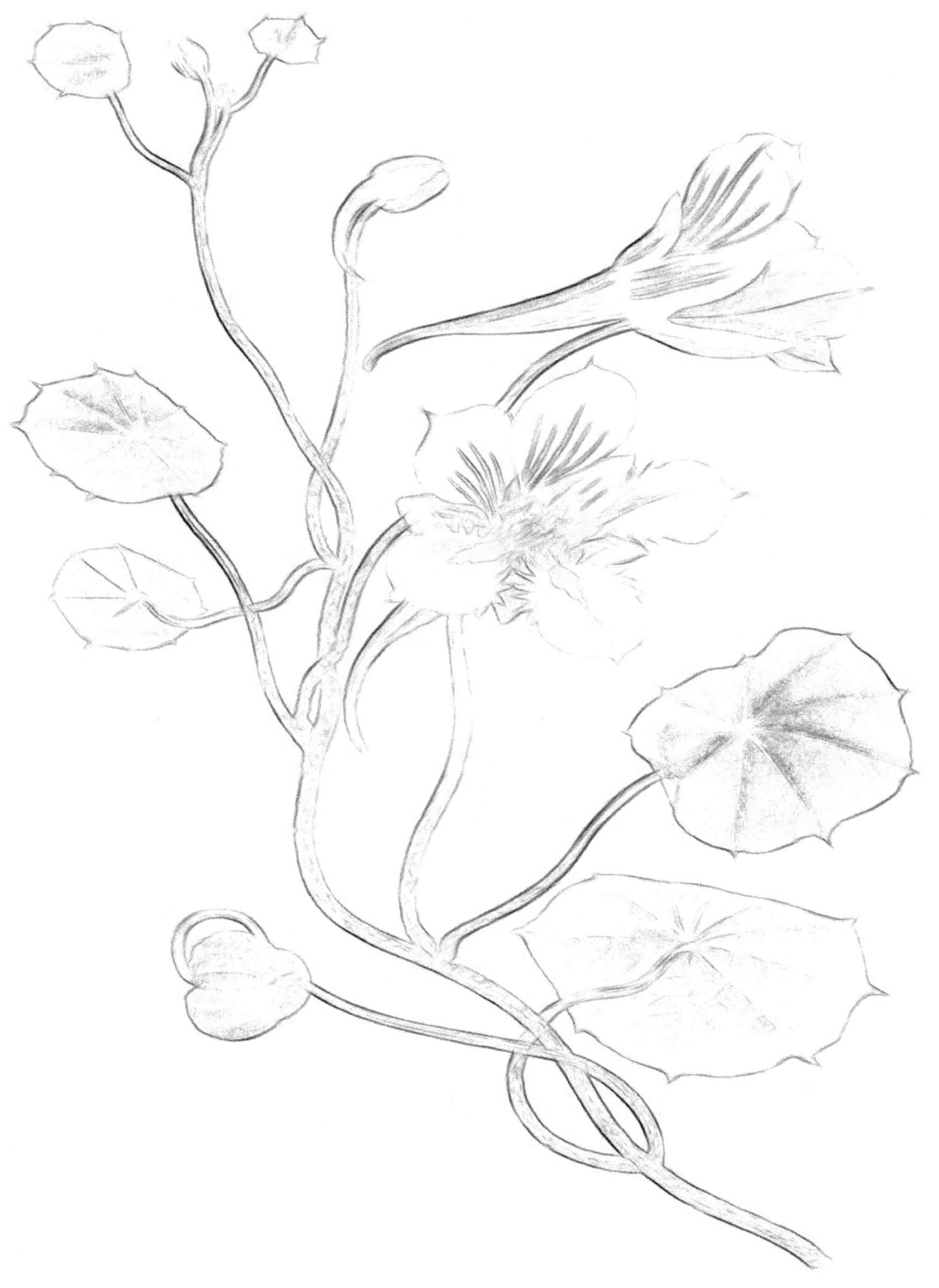

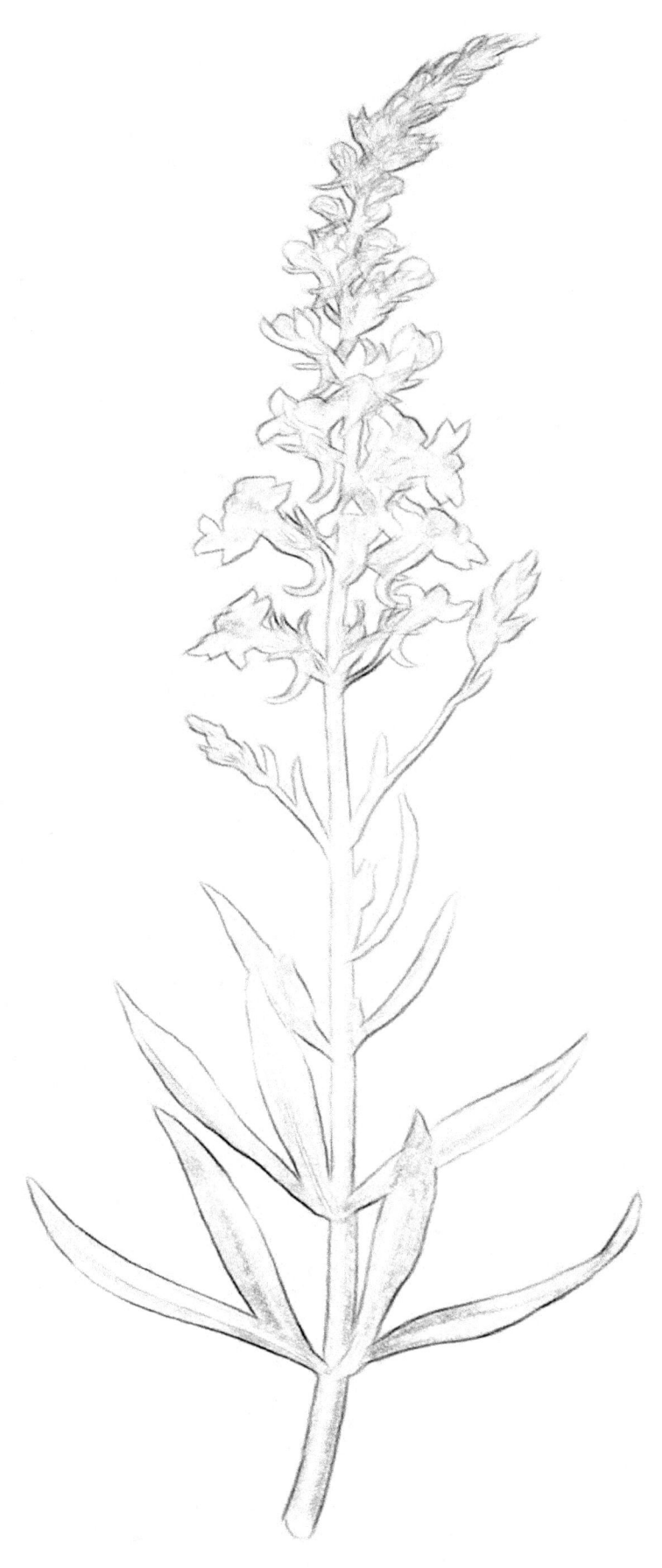

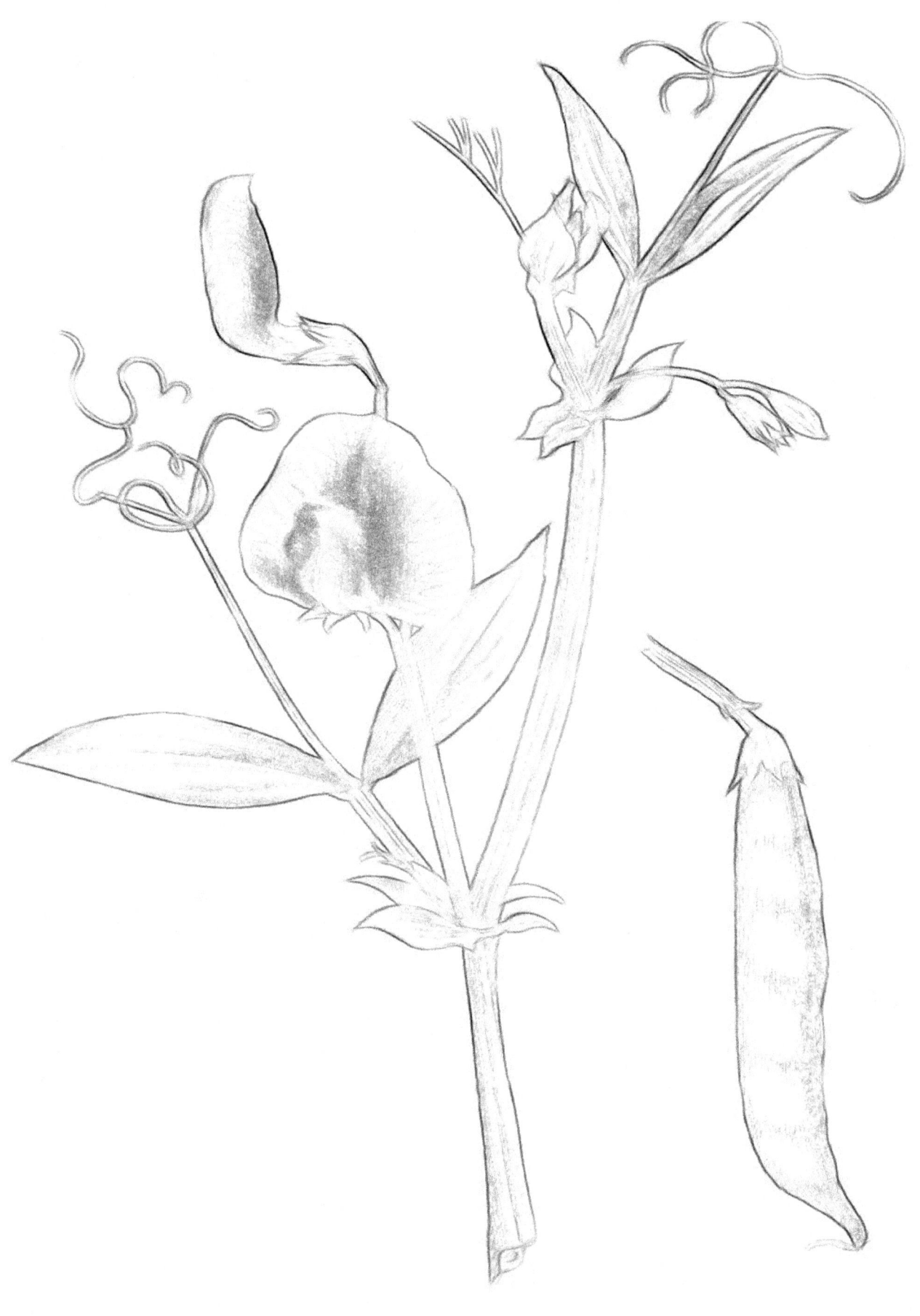

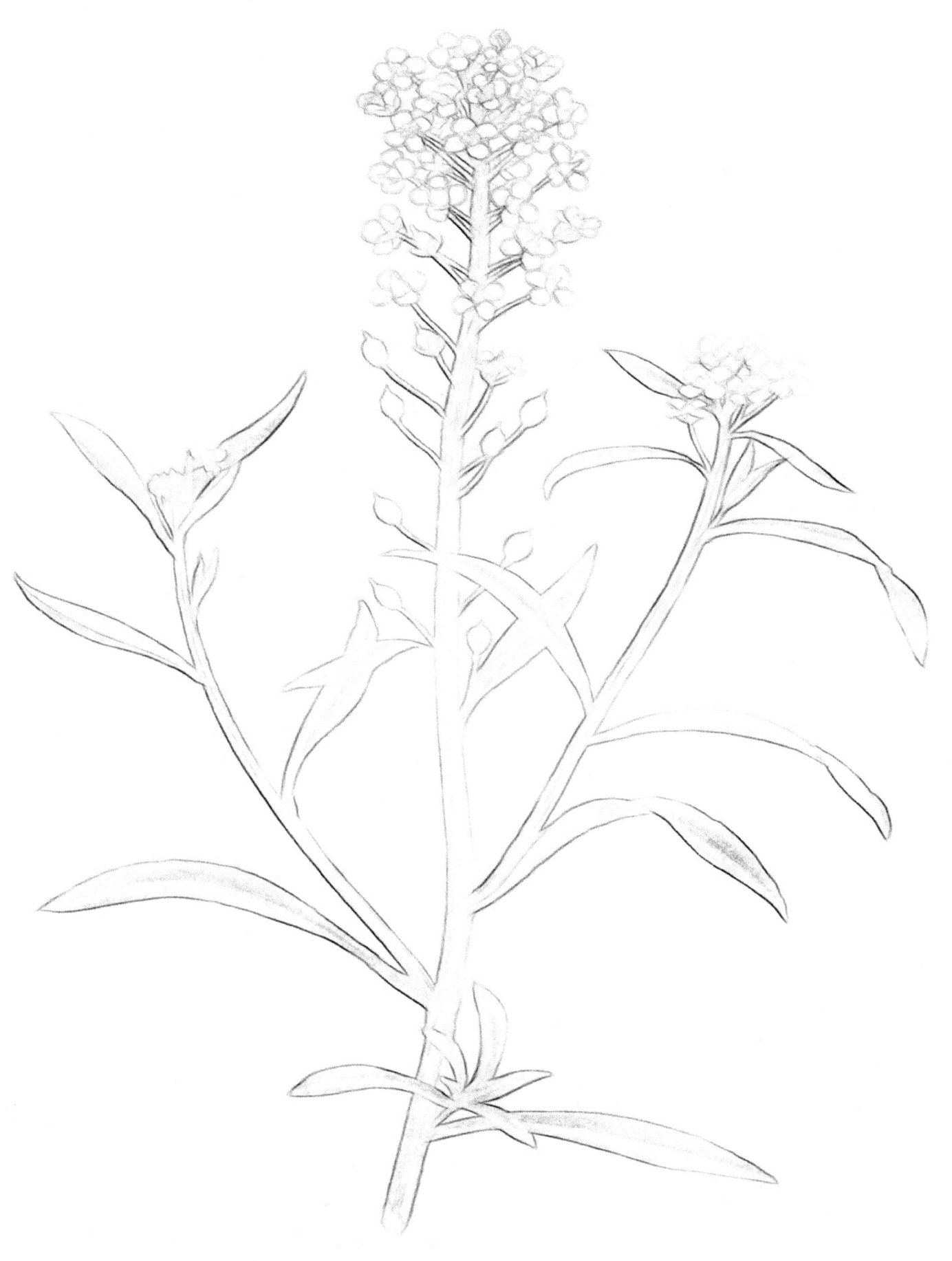

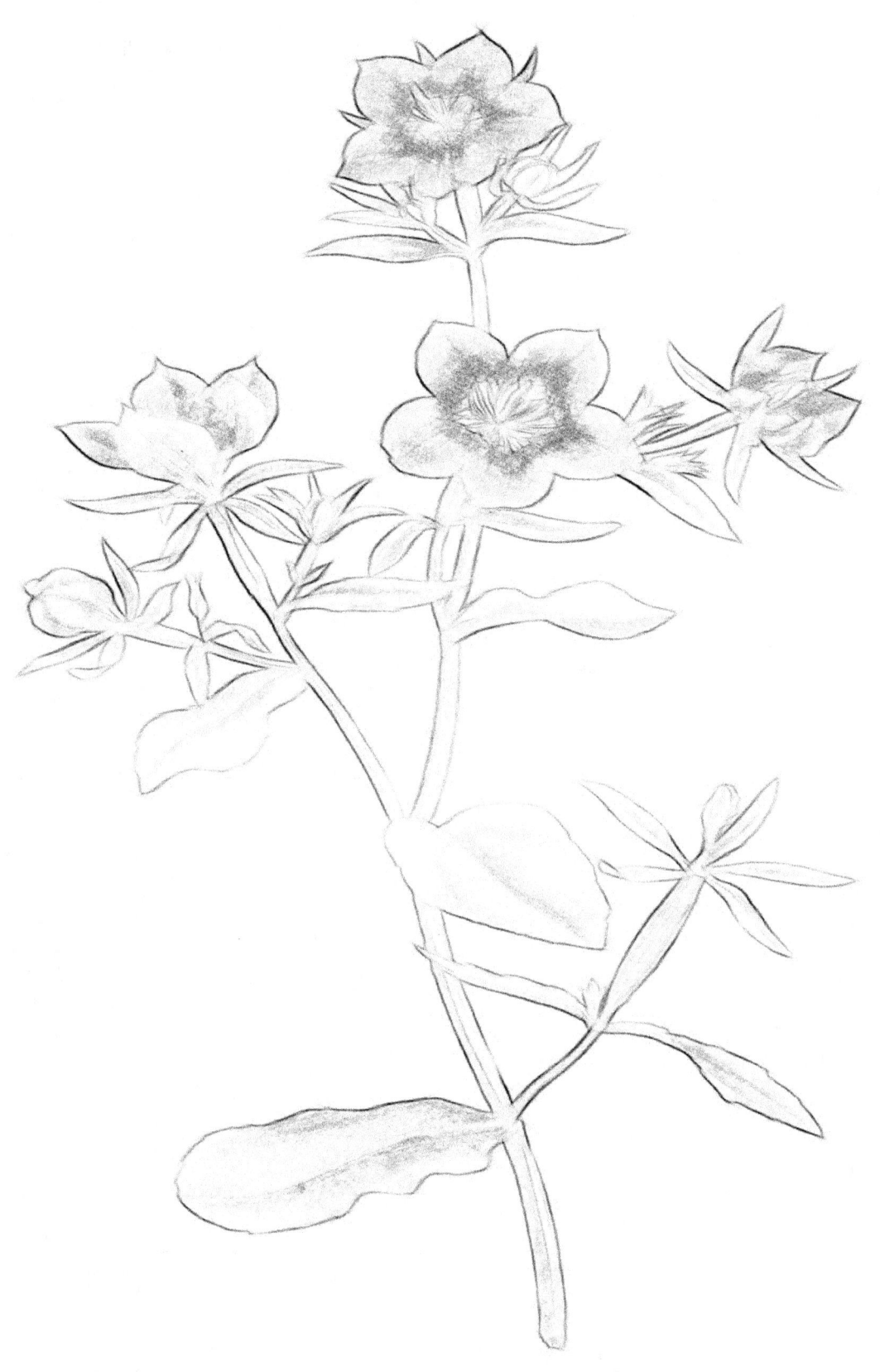

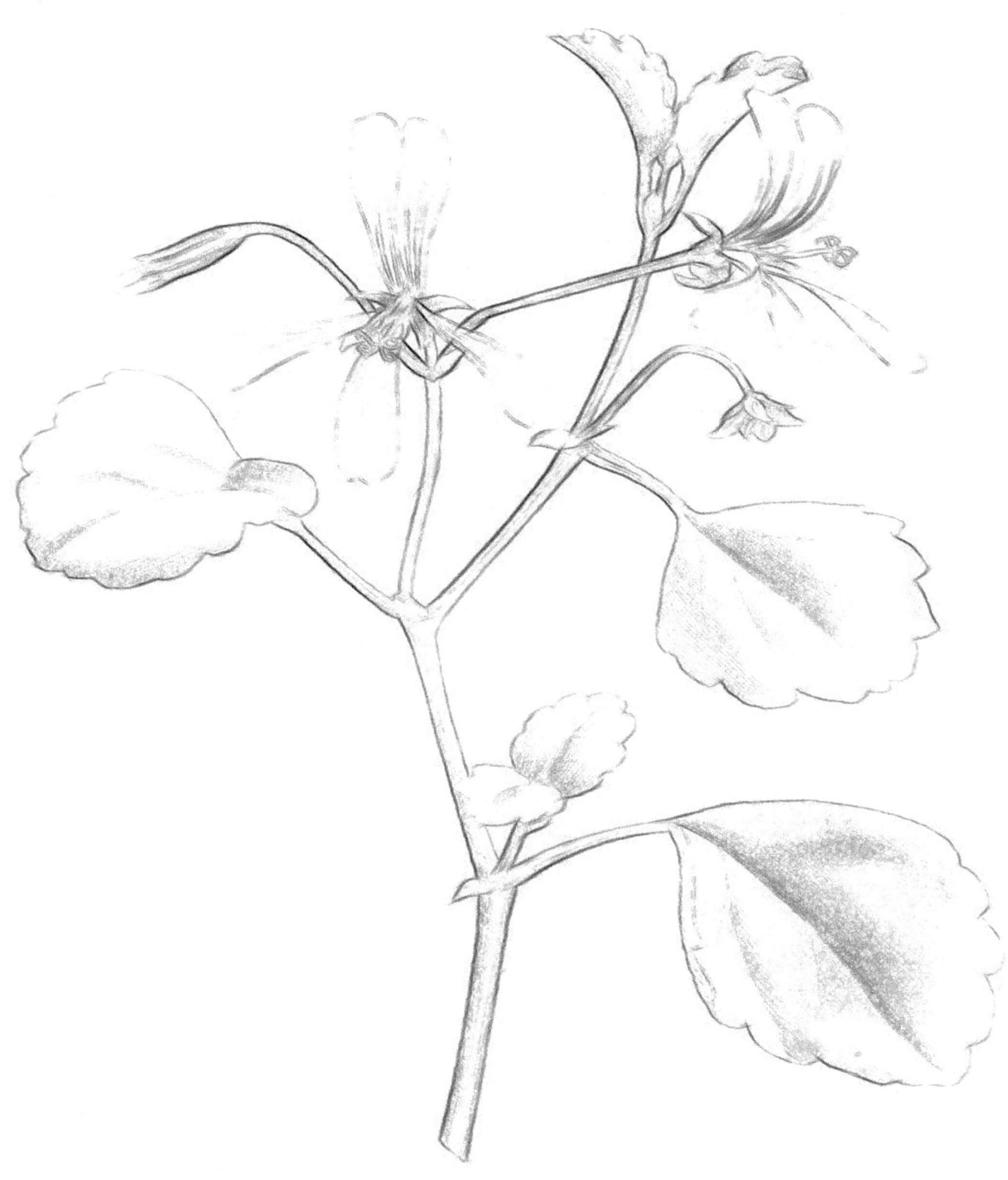

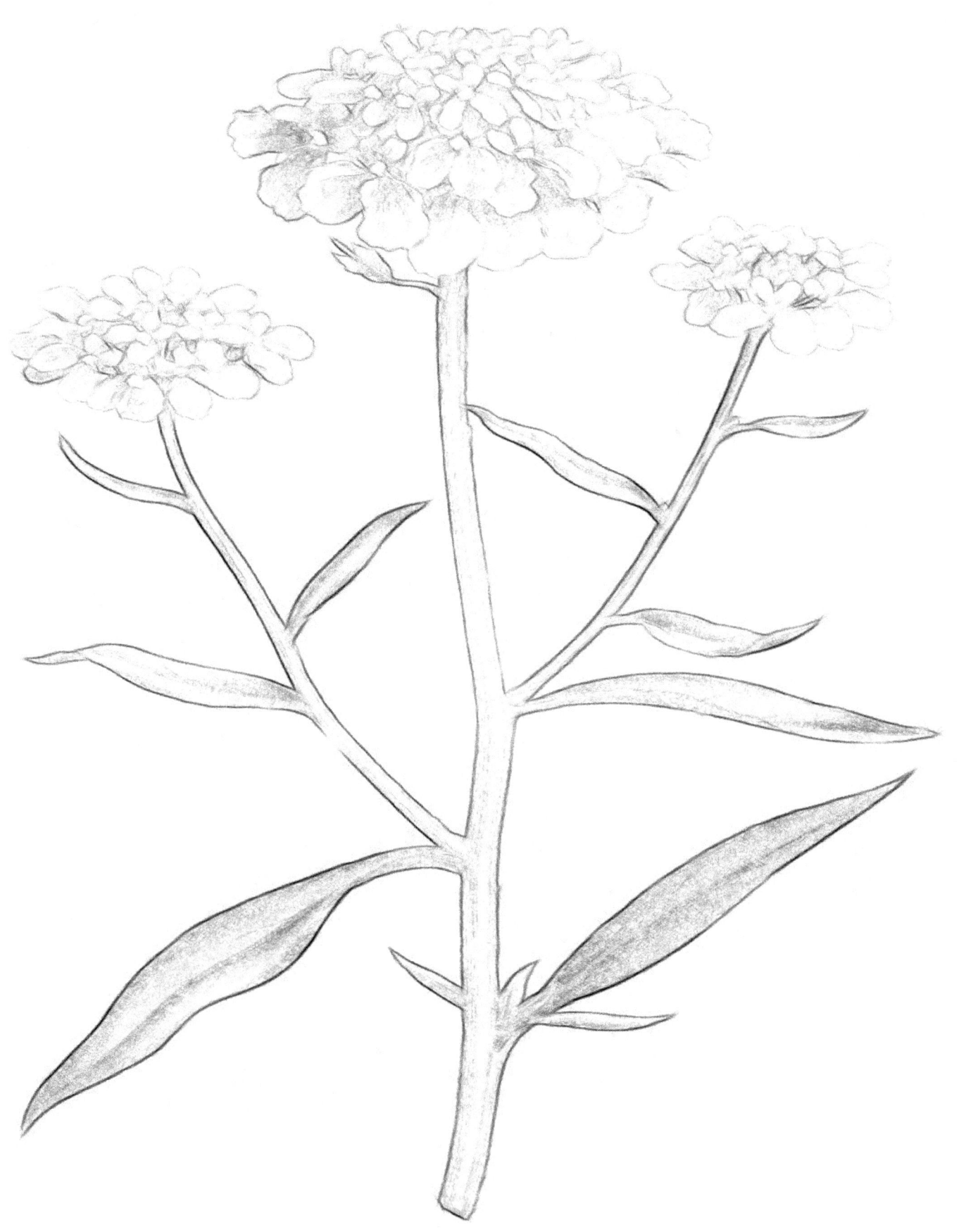

www.ingramcontent.com/pod-product-compliance
Lightning Source LLC
Chambersburg PA
CBHW081621170526
45166CB00009B/3065